Teaching Mii

to

Children & Teens

Katharine Ardel

Elisabeth Rose Wilds

A Brighter Light in the World

A Brighter Light in the World®

Our brand, A Brighter Light in the World® focuses on creating children's books, novels, self-help books and guided meditation CDs that are designed for those walking a spiritual path. The inspiration for the brand comes from a diversity of traditions with the hope to share these voices of wisdom from our past and spark a light that brings us all to a greater place of harmony.

For updates on new products and events, please visit our web site at www.thehealingartscenter.org and our Facebook Page, A Brighter Light in the World, or follow us on Twitter @A_BrighterLight.

The cover image was created by Natalia Tretiakova. Please visit our web site to learn more about Natalia's work.

This book was thoughtfully edited by Mary G. Belmore.

ISBN-10: 1-466-319-47X
ISBN-13: 978-1-466-319-479

CONTENTS

PREFACE

Mindfulness is a practice that helps us quiet the mind and improve the quality of our life and our ability to appreciate the many gifts that we have been blessed with.

Elisabeth and Kathie designed this book with simplicity in mind, focusing on techniques and practices that can be easily incorporated into daily living – knowing from experience that it doesn't have to be difficult to work!

As you begin to walk this path, step gently and with patience, appreciating the fullness of the moment that this practice will bestow upon you and your family.

INTRODUCTION

Aspects of mindfulness practice have been present in our culture and our daily lives for many generations. These practices were associated with an era that had fewer distractions from TV, computers and overbooked schedules. Focus and concentration were required to complete many of our tasks. When most jobs such as preparing food, washing clothes, sewing, or chopping wood were done by hand, we had to pay attention to what we were doing. Our lives shared a deeper connection with nature.

Today, aspects of mindfulness practice are very much a part of the revitalization of the artisan culture, which focuses on creating products by hand, the old-fashioned way.

However, mindfulness moves beyond simply paying attention to what you are doing. It gives you and your children the opportunity to live from a deeper and more authentic place inside – developing a quality of presence that fosters peace and compassion, and a greater appreciation for the natural world.

We hope that this book gives you some ideas on how to incorporate an attitude of mindfulness into your day, every day.

What is Mindfulness?

- o Mindfulness is the awareness that our thoughts impact our well-being.

- o Mindfulness practice involves observing our thoughts and noticing our reactions to those thoughts.

- o Ultimately, the practice of mindfulness empowers us to choose thoughts that serve a higher good.

The Benefits of Practicing Mindfulness

- o Mindfulness develops our ability to remain centered and respond from the quiet, sacred place within.

- o Mindfulness helps us to see the infinite possibilities of every situation, giving us the opportunity to interact in healthier ways, rather than through conditioned responses.

- o It is a practice that develops our ability to interact with an open heart, improving our ability to listen compassionately.

- o Mindfulness helps us to step out of the stories we create that cause us fear and worry.

MINDFULNESS FOR OUR CHILDREN

This segment introduces the components of mindfulness practice on a step-by-step basis. It will offer ways of using the elements of the natural world as a way of experiencing moments of peace and inner harmony.

Practice that can be easily inserted within your child's day will be offered after each segment that introduces ways of teaching your child to re-balance and self-regulate when they are suffering from stormy emotions.

This section ends with ways that storytelling can be a wonderful tool to reinforce mindfulness practices for your child.

And now begin the joyful journey of Mindfulness...

Teaching Stillness

By teaching stillness we create moments
for our children to rebalance.
Stillness is a natural response
when we observe nature.

Silence falls upon us,
our breath slows,
and
our heart opens.

As we enter the frequency of nature,
we experience inner harmony.

These moments of stillness
become the pauses
within our children's days
that allow them to momentarily reset
and once again find inner balance.

Stillness is a natural response
as we observe nature.

And for this reason,
the easiest and most natural way
to teach stillness
is by taking the time to observe
the natural world around us.

Take a moment
to think of how we find ourselves
completely still and quiet
as we watch a rabbit nibble
on a patch of grass.

As soon as the words,
"Look over there!" are uttered
in reference to some fauna or flora,
silence falls upon us.

We stop talking and look.
Not only does our mind become quiet,
but our body becomes still.

Why is this?
Is this simply old programming
that our modern world has not yet erased?

Or is it something deeper?

Have we awakened
our primordial spirit
as we find ourselves once again
in tune with
the rhythms of the natural world?

Practice

<u>The One Minute Pause</u>

We need only to create moments
in our children's lives
to notice and observe nature
- and stillness comes.

This can be as simple as stopping the car
on the way to a lesson,
to observe a beautiful tree
or a beautiful moment in nature.

It can be stopping on the front steps
on our way out to listen to a bird.

Just one minute.

The One Minute Pause
that deepens our love.

Make Time

Make time
to watch a sunset or sunrise,
a grasshopper climbing a blade of grass,
the shape of the clouds overhead,

the path of an ant on pavement,
the dance of tree limbs in the breeze,
the brightness of the moon,
the flight of a leaf as it falls to the ground,
and
to listen to the song of birds,
the rustle of leaves,
the patter of rainfall,
the gusts of a stormy breeze,
and
to feel the warmth of the sun,
the softness of your pet's fur,
and
the wind as it tickles your toes.

Finding That Peaceful Place Within

Teaching stillness
with the simple 'One Minute Pause'
introduces our children
to a peaceful place within.

As the mind's chatter falls away,
they are able to observe
from a deeper place inside.

This is the sacred place of
ritual, of prayer, and of meditation

We are gifting them with
a moment of being fully present in the world –
focused, alert, engaged,
yet relaxed and at peace.

We are teaching them
a way of relating that does not involve 'ego'
- but simply presence.

A presence in perfect harmony
is truly a gift to behold.

This is the gift of nature.

What a powerful antidote
to the maze of emotions and dramas
that arise from our interactions throughout the day.

Practice

<u>Share Love with the World</u>

One way of guiding our children
to the peaceful place of their inner world
is to suggest sharing
their love with the natural world.

Have them send their love to a small bird
perched in a tree.
Take a moment to honor that gift.

Have them send their love to the tree
in the backyard or the park.
Remember to pause in stillness
as this beautiful gift is sent and received.

This practice opens the door for conversation
on opening our heart and sharing our love
and the many miracles
that come through this practice.

Discuss the feelings and sensations
that arise when we share our love with the world.

Practice

Water Blessing

The ritual of water blessing is a similar exercise.
It is an offering of love to the world.

Using water to do blessing work
is a wonderful way
to integrate the concept of our connection
with the natural world
and how important it is for our well-being.

Have your children bless the water they drink,
or bless the water that is used for plants,
or bless the water for their bath.

For older children, ages 4 and up,
the book
The Secret of Water
by Dr. Masaru Emoto
is a wonderful way for children
to learn how their love
positively impacts the formation of water crystals
and the world around them.

Developing the Observer

The observer is a part of ourselves that is aware of our
thoughts, actions and words.
This is the part that simply watches.
The observer gifts us with inner awareness.

As we begin to look at our thoughts
as simply thoughts,
we develop a different perspective.

We suddenly realize
that we are
much, much more
than our thoughts.

We can recognize the observer
with the simple questions:

Who is thinking all those thoughts?
Where are they coming from?

Be content with the concept that
'Thoughts Arise.'

Whether or not we choose to take notice
of our thoughts is totally in our hands.
It is a choice.

As we practice observing our thoughts,
we develop discernment.

Soon we discover that many of our thoughts
are simply distractions
that keep us mentally occupied
and unable to enjoy the present moment.

Advanced souls living amongst us
refer to our thoughts
as birds flying over head
that need not disturb us,
unless we reach for them.

However, when temptation strikes
and we reach for a thought,
the emotional roller coaster ride begins.

We have just created a nest for the bird,
a story that is only happening within ourselves.

A story that impacts our well-being,
as our body believes every word.

Practice

Thought Observation

Become aware of your thoughts
and which ones you choose to feed.
Which thoughts bring a smile to your face?
Which thoughts keep you agitated
and restless?

Keep tabs on what 'mind' is thinking.

How many of those thoughts
create distractions that send you spiraling down
an unpleasant journey
where the ending is never satisfactory
regardless of the multiple scenarios
you create?

And consider for a moment,
the possibility that you have a choice
of what you choose to think about.

And how your choice of thought
could create
changes in your well-being
and
healthier responses to the world around you.

Practice

Happy Thoughts

When you have spent some time
developing your observer,
share with your children
one of your happy thoughts.

Let them know how it makes you feel.
Be descriptive of thought and feeling -
"My face makes a beautiful smile
and I feel warm and tingly inside."

Then ask them which thoughts make them happy,
and where they feel the happiness inside.

Asking children what 'mind' is up to
is another way to help them develop the observer.

The Mind-Body Connection

Awareness of the mind-body connection
helps to develop mindfulness.

Practice

Body Observation

When your child is upset, ask them where they feel
that 'upset' in their body.
Ask them if that part of their body feels
hot, cold, tight, itchy, heavy, etc.

Giving them a moment to investigate their body
allows them the opportunity
to step into the observer mode.

Ask them how they can make that part
of their body feel better.

Does it need a hug?
A kind word?
A gentle rub?
Some love sent there?

By doing this exercise, they are learning
to self-regulate, and it gives them the opportunity
to regain their balance while shifting into
the role of the observer.

Taking Mind-Body Awareness to the Next Level

Times of upset may become teaching moments,
if you have already introduced
mindfulness practices,
and more importantly,
if you, the parent, are in a calm state of mind.

When an upsetting situation happens,
of course your child will go into
an emotional state
with the accompanying behavior.

When the 'crisis' begins to pass and
once the child is calmer,
a discussion can follow where
'the story is analyzed'
and all the thoughts that arose with it.

At this time, alternative responses or ways of looking at
things can be introduced.
With the caveat - how would that make you feel?

By creating alternative responses to a situation,
you are teaching healthier ways
of being in the world.

By asking "How would that make you feel?"
you are teaching the child to take ownership
of feelings and emotions
and demonstrating that we do indeed have power
over how we feel and relate to the world.

Bringing consciousness to a level
where we begin
to experiment with how our interpretation
of situations impacts us,
is a powerful tool
to share with our children.

Use common sense.

Not all situations will go smoothly.

If your child is angry or upset for not getting
his or her way,
you can certainly go through the steps
of identifying where emotions
are being expressed in the body.

This gives your child the opportunity to
step into the observer mode,
which may help them to rebalance.

15

Your child may not be able to shift
into a more enlightened view of the situation.

Keep in mind that
you are planting seeds of understanding,
and in time that understanding will grow.

On some level your child is learning
that his or her perception
is creating the suffering he or she is experiencing.

Being a calm presence can be a beautiful gift
to your child when he or she is struggling
with strong emotions.

And if appropriate, with kindness remind your child
that a bright sunny sky with no tears
is always within their reach -
just as close as their next happy thought.

Focusing on the Breath

Breathing is essential to life,
Yet rarely are we aware that we are doing it -
every moment.
When we bring mindfulness to the breath
we bring awareness to an essential
motion of our living being.

So by bringing mindfulness
to the breath,
We bring mindfulness
into our life.

Practice

Breathe Together

This can be a profound experience.
It would be good to practice
with your partner or spouse
before teaching your child.

Sit or stand facing your child.
Try to be at the same eye level.
Hold both hands very gently.
Eyes may be open or closed.
Either way breathing together is bonding.

With the eyes open, one can feel very vulnerable,
yet with a loved one looking into your eyes,
it is a moment of recognizing unconditional love.

Breathe together, letting the body relax.
When you are sharing this with a child,
the child will naturally entrain
to your state of being.

Because relaxation can be a challenge for adults,
when you first start this practice,
you might want to listen to soft music
or consciously begin a relaxation process -
where you let the facial muscles relax,
then the neck and shoulders,
and then allow
the back, the legs and the arms to soften.

18

Breathe slowly together.
Try it with closed eyes, then with open eyes.

Let the breathing come into synchronization.
It happens all by itself.
Sharing love in this simple way is a divine miracle.
Both will feel blessed.

This exercise can be used to calm an upset child.
When you participate, you will find that
your own upset is calmed as well.

This is a good time to have the eyes closed.
Closing the eyes
and
maintaining an awareness of the breath
encourages us to go INSIDE
and
become Quiet.

Storytelling

Storytelling is a powerful tool.
For centuries it was the primary way that
cultural values and knowledge were transmitted
from one generation to the next.

Practice

Create a Story

Give your child the opportunity to create
his or her own story where they are the main character.

This is a wonderful way to teach mindfulness,
develop the observer, and have your child experiment
with different responses to situations.

As an active listener, you can insert pauses into the story
where the character has a moment
to reflect or center themselves
before emotions run wild
in the adventure or misadventure your child creates.

You can question your child's judgment
and ask why they chose this way or that.

And, if the child is mature enough,
ask how a different response may have changed the story.

"What would happen if the character got angry, or scared,
or just laughed at the monster?"

Consider inserting a character that is very wise.
Ask your child what advice that character
may have for the main character.

And without taking too much of the fun out
of your child's creation,
ask your child what the character learned
from their adventure.

Storytelling Taken to the Next Level

In life, we have the facts of a situation
and we have our 'story' about it.

When we change the 'story' we hold,
then the feelings and psychological affects
of an event change.

It is a matter of choosing our thoughts
about the situation
that changes the long-term effects
it may have on our lives.

For example, Mary's little brother was allowed
to hit her whenever he wanted a toy
that she was playing with.

Mary could hold onto this story as an excuse
for having low self-esteem.

Or she could take a larger view and realize
that from this experience
she learned about 'selfishness'
and how
it creates disharmony and discord
in the world.

By doing this, she is stepping out
of the victim mode
and stepping forward
into a more compassionate view
that no longer personalizes her brother's behavior.

By doing so, she is freeing herself
from thoughts
that impact her sense of self-worth.

MINDFULNESS FOR OUR TEENS

This segment opens the door for communication with your teenager by addressing the relevance of mindfulness practice in today's society by showing the value it brings to many professions.

The connection between stress and fearful thoughts is discussed with suggestions on ways to reclaim our natural state of peacefulness by simple exercises that help quiet the mind.

It shows that we have choices in what we think and what stories we create. It investigates our body's responses to the stories we create and discusses the use of visualization to assist us forward in healthier ways of being in the world.

Mindfulness in the World Today

Your teenager will want to understand
how mindfulness practice will be useful for them
in achieving their goals.

Try sharing a conversation investigating
the value of being present in the professional world
and how mental distractions
have the potential to create disaster.

Certain professions require
mental focus, alertness, and clarity.
Discuss the possible outcomes
of mental distractions for the following professions:

Fire fighter
Race car driver
Dentist
Surgeon
Athlete
Scientist
Welder
Stunt man
Performer

If your teenager is into sports,
you may want to talk about
"being in the zone"
and what that means.
And how one trains to achieve that state.

Reclaiming our Peace

It is important for your teenager
to understand that
our natural state is one of peacefulness.

It is also important for them
to begin to see
the connection between stress and their thoughts.

If you ask your teenager what is causing their stress,
they will come up with a very long list.
Attentively listen to them.

Some teenagers will perceive
that it is their fearful thoughts and worries
that are creating their stress.

If they haven't gotten there yet,
ask them if they would have stress
if they stopped thinking.

They may consider this a trick question.
Or you may hear the response,
"It is impossible to stop thinking!"
Or even, "If you stop thinking, you will die!"

These discussions usually trigger
some interest
in the connection between the mind and stress.

It is usually helpful at this juncture
to talk about practices
that your teenager may have heard of
that help quiet the mind.

More than likely, they will surprise you
with their knowledge of yoga or meditation.

The Untrained Mind

An untrained mind is a very active thinker.

The enlightened among us describe
the untrained mind's behavior to be like a puppy
that we have just brought home.
It runs all over the house,
bringing chaos in its wake.

In order to train the puppy properly,
we need to have patience and some firmness.

Anger and frustration don't help us.
We simply need to be consistent in our efforts of bringing
the puppy back to its room or rug.

Just like the puppy, the untrained mind will have a difficult
time focusing on one thing,
and will want to run around here and there.
It is our job to bring the mind back
to what we are focusing on.

There are different methods that are used
to assist the mind in focusing on one thing.

Some practices use a mantra,
while others may use the breath,
and still others may use the concentrated effort
of slowly rehearsed movements,
like those found in tai chi chuan.

Practice

Guided Meditation

A pleasant way to begin the process of training the mind
is to introduce your teenager to guided meditation CDs,
preferably ones with a storyline or guided journey,
which will assist in keeping the mind somewhat occupied,
but focused on one topic.

It is always best to listen to the guided meditation
beforehand so that you can see how it impacts you
and if it is suitable for your teenager.

Listening to the guided meditation with your teenager
would be wonderful, if that works for you.

As your teenager listens to the guided meditation,
suggest that they visualize the story as best they can
and when they notice their mind beginning to wander,
suggest that they bring it back to the story.

Ask your teenager if they were able to visit
the places in the story
and if they noticed any change
in their breathing, body or stress level.

Noticing how the body responds to the story
is one of the first steps in understanding
the mind-body connection.

At this time, you may want to ask your teenager
how the body might respond
to stories that are not so pleasant,
or stories that are upsetting.

Comment on how the body seems to believe everything
we tell it and responds accordingly.

If your teenager falls asleep during the guided meditation,
let them sleep.

Asleep or awake, the state of relaxation that they will be
experiencing through this process
will be wonderful for their well-being.

The Observer

The observer is developed by taking a moment to pause
with our outward activities
and notice the thoughts
running through our mind.

Pausing may be difficult to do as many of us live our lives
by lists, schedules and deadlines.

When you take a moment to check in,
notice your level of restlessness.
How fast is your heart rate?
Become aware of your breath.
Are there any tensions or pain in your body?

Remind yourself that this precious moment,
this pause in your sea of activities
is a step in your journey to find greater harmony within.
Honor the moment and honor your practice.

There is a process of discernment that comes
from determining what thoughts
we need to notice and take note of
and those that are simply distractions
or habitual thinking patterns.

Becoming aware of disturbing or troubling thoughts that
repeatedly present themselves
could indicate a need to seek counseling.

If your teenager notices that a particular thought
disturbs them or makes them feel uncomfortable,
suggest that they talk about it with
a family member or counselor.

Explain to your teenager that they need not
be terrorized by their thoughts.

Developing the observer helps teenagers recognize

"This thought is driving me crazy,"

versus,

"I can't take this anymore."

Practice

Breath Observation

If your teenager has developed a degree of discipline
from sports, music, the arts or studying,
you may want to introduce an exercise where they sit
quietly and focus on their breath.

Have them notice the difference in temperature as it enters
and leaves the body.
This is very apparent when we are breathing
through the nose.
Have them notice if their breath is shallow
or if their belly moves with it.
Have them follow their breath mentally
through their body.

During this exercise,
which can be practiced for as little as one minute,
suggest that your teenager notice
the thoughts that come up,
allow the thought,
but then bring the mind back to the breath.

Ask them if the exercise became easier
over time or more difficult.

If the one minute of practice time
felt much longer,
question to what extent brain activity
may impact our perception of time.

Many of us have felt time move slowly
when we have been asked
to hold a difficult posture,
hold our breath,
or even wait in line!

Ask your teenager if it is possible that the mind,
like the other parts of the body,
needs to trained
in order to build stamina, focus and concentration.

See if there is any interest on the part of your teenager
to attempt this exercise on a more regular basis,
and what they hope they may achieve by doing so.

Remember you are planting seeds,
so it is best not to have expectations.

Your gift is sharing ideas and being fully present.

Interacting and truly listening to your teenager
can be a very healing experience for everyone.

Hooking Thoughts

It is important for your teenager to understand that
'thoughts' in and of themselves
cannot harm them.

Learning to pause and observe their thoughts
will help your teenager begin to understand that
'thoughts come' and 'thoughts go.'

And it is only when we 'hook' a thought
that we empower it –
once we hook a thought,
the thought can take us on an emotional ride
that is solely dependent on the story
we create with the thought that we have hooked.

We create stories.
These stories can cause us to experience
uplifting emotions,
or become utterly discouraged,
or believe that we are the perpetual victim
of an uncomfortable situation
from many years ago.

When we tell ourselves stories,
our bodies react to the mind's vision of reality,
not knowing that it is simply a story
occurring nowhere,
except in our mind.

Talking about post-traumatic stress symptoms
is a way for your teenager to relate
how the body responds to our thoughts.

A relevant topic would be a car accident,
where the survivor becomes afraid of driving
or riding in a car again.

Ask your teenager, what types of physical symptoms
the survivor might possibly feel?

Ask your teenager, what types of thoughts,
conscious or unconscious,
might be responsible for creating
some of those symptoms?

These types of examples help your teenager understand
that our body is very obedient
and responds to our thoughts.

Your teenager is learning at some level
that our body obediently responds
to what we are telling it,
whether the response is from an actual thought
or a cue – visual, sound or touch.

Let your teenager know that there are methods that are
used to assist people
in recovering from post-traumatic stress symptoms.
It need not be a lifelong struggle.

Storytelling

By developing the observer,
we can get in touch with our stories.

Most of us are not able to jump into a state of "no-mind"
and enjoy a complete restful silence -
here is a way that we can work with our mind
to improve our well-being.

We can consciously tell ourselves beautiful stories.

Stories that lead us to our favorite beach,
garden, or park bench.
We can imagine the gentle breeze,
the birds singing, and a beautiful sky.
Images that make us feel at ease and at peace.

We can create mental images to support ourselves
through difficult times,
an image where we give ourselves a big hug
and words of encouragement.

Creating these types of positive imagery
helps to restore our inner balance
and can be wonderful in relieving tension and stress.

Practice

Share Your Story

Take time to become familiar with your
own mental habits and stories.

And, then take the time
to create a few of your own beautiful stories
that you can share with your teenager.
And let them know how these stories make you feel.

When you talk to your teenager,
the word they may be familiar with is visualization.

Ask them if they have heard how athletes
use visualization in their training.
Ask them if they have used visualization
to achieve a personal goal.

Ask your teenager if there is a visualization
that they use which helps them
when they are under stress.

Listening to your teenager with sincere interest
will create an environment for them
to share their own ideas and experiences.

Listening with sincere interest,
quiets the mind and creates a sacred space
for unlimited possibilities and responses.

Sharing time with your teenager is precious.

Some teenagers will assume that
questions are a form of interrogation.

If this describes your teenager,
try simply sharing your own responses
to a guided meditation.

Some teens may go through a period of
"I have a stupid parent."

If this is your situation,
finding a teen yoga, tai-chi or meditation class
is heavenly!

SHARED REMARKS

Mindfulness is not something new.

However, in America,
with our hectic and materialistic lifestyle,
it has been ignored.

In the name of achievement and progress,
we have neglected our Peace of Mind.

It is wonderful when parents
with a calm and well-disciplined mind,
a healthy emotional system
with a strong spiritual foundation
can raise their babies and toddlers,
children and teenagers
in a serene loving environment.

However, this is not what most of us start out with.
Often it is not until we have children
that we begin to see the need for serenity.

So many parents get to learn
as they teach their children the way of mindfulness.

Fortunately, mindfulness is now encouraged
by our emerging spiritual evolution.

Popular authors and even talk show hosts are making
mindfulness a common word and worthy effort.

Mindfulness includes compassion, attention, peace,
appropriateness and responsibility.

Is a past memory thought worth your peace of mind?
Once you can OBSERVE the thought,
you can choose to LET IT GO.

Will a coffee spill ruin your day?
Or can you simply clean it up?
It is always YOUR CHOICE.

Is a mistake of another driver worth
your peaceful ride to school with your child?
Once you OBSERVE your reaction,
You can choose to LET IT GO.

Do we teach mindfulness to our kids?
It may be more accurate to say that
we SHARE mindfulness.

Sharing mindfully with our loved ones
is a responsibility of relationship.

Our children will learn to live the way we do.
Children learn to live in this world first by imitation.

When a child sees inner peace,
that child learns inner peace.

This is WHY it is so important to integrate
these simple lessons into life every day.

Your baby, your child and your teenager
watch and learn to live the way you do.

The benefits of mindfulness are beyond measure.

Mindfulness places sacred attention
on what brings joy and peace
into our lives.

RESOURCES

There are many wonderful resources to support your journey on the path of mindfulness. You will find this topic discussed by spiritual leaders of the yogic and Buddhist traditions, as well as in early Christian dogma written by the Desert Fathers. This path is also familiar to and practiced by native and indigenous peoples from around the world. Choose a tradition that resonates with you.

There is a wonderful blog called storygins.com that gives parents ideas on how to teach their children through storytelling.

Our brand, A Brighter Light in the World® focuses on creating children's books, novels, self-help books and guided meditation CDs that are designed for those walking a spiritual path. The inspiration for the brand's products comes from a diversity of traditions with the hope to share these voices of wisdom from our past and spark a light that brings us all to a greater place of harmony.

Our children's books on mindfulness are *We Are Like the Sky*, and soon to be released *The Adventures of Body, Mind and Spirit – That Rascal!* and *Cookie's Magical Snow*.

Our books on opening the heart and connecting with nature are *Rainbow of Light, We Play Beautiful Music*, and *Blessing the Water*, to be followed by *I Am* and *Hugging My Tree*.

Mystra and the Way of the Keepers is a fantasy novel, where seekers of truth struggle to solve a mystery, assisted by wizards, elves and higher beings. On this spiritual quest they are challenged to grow and transform beyond anything they could have ever imagined.

Our guided meditation CD series focuses on stories that assist us in addressing the developmental issues of each of the seven major chakras. The music follows the storyline and is specifically designed to energetically support the listener through each journey. Our guided meditation CDs are *EMBRACING – The First Chakra* and *BECOMING – The Second Chakra*.

BIOGRAPHIES

Katharine Ardel

Katharine earned her doctoral degree from the American Institute of Hypnotherapy and teaches Basic and Advanced Hypnotherapy courses. She is a Reiki Master and teacher of the Incan Tradition of Shamanic Healing, Yoga and Metaphysics. In addition, Kathie presents personal growth workshops nationally.

Kathie has extensive experience working with children and teenagers. She managed a day care center and directed recreational youth programs for several years, in addition to raising her two daughters.

Kathie has a strong background in social services working with high risk teens in prevention programs. She integrates guided imagery into her work with teenagers and clients.

Elisabeth Rose Wilds

Elisabeth has studied healing modalities in the Far Eastern, Native American and Andean traditions over the past twenty years. Elisabeth founded and administers a Healing Arts Center at a non-profit organization in New York City focused on assisting homeless youths. In addition, she teaches classes in personal development, stress management, mindfulness and the healing arts.

A Brighter Light in the World®
Products based on the Healing Arts

Children's Books

Rainbow of Light
We Play Beautiful Music
Blessing the Water
We Are Like the Sky
The Adventures of Body, Mind & Spirit - That Rascal!
Cookie's Magical Snow
Hugging My Tree
I Am

Guided Meditation CDs & MP3s

EMBRACING - The First Chakra
BECOMING - The Second Chakra

Novel & eBook

Mystra and the Way of the Keepers

A Brighter Light in the World®
products are available for purchase at Our Store on
our web site www.thehealingartscenter.org
and at your local bookseller.

Printed in Great Britain
by Amazon